A Visit to
THE
UNITED KINGDOM

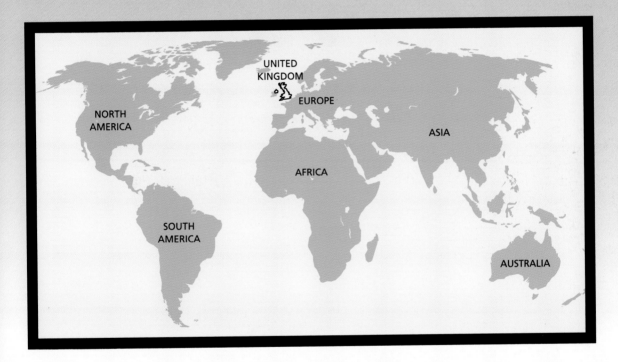

UNITED
KINGDOM

EUROPE

NORTH
AMERICA

ASIA

AFRICA

SOUTH
AMERICA

AUSTRALIA

Rachael Bell

Heinemann Library
Des Plaines, Illinois

Designed by AMR
Illustrations by Art Construction
Printed and bound in Hong Kong/China by South China Printing Co.

03 02 01 00 99
10 9 8 7 6 5 4 3 2 1

Library of Congress Cataloging-in-Publication Data

Bell, Rachael, 1972-
    The United Kingdom / Rachael Bell.
        p. cm.
    Includes bibliographical references and index.
    Summary: Introduces the land, landmarks, homes, food, clothing, work, transportation, language, and culture of the United Kingdom.
        ISBN 1-57572-846-X (lib. bdg.)
    1. Great Britain—Juvenile literature. 2. Ireland—Juvenile literature. [1. Great Britain. 2. Ireland.] I. Title. II. Series
    DA27.5.B45 1999
    941—dc21   98-45091
                                                  CIP
                                                  AC

Acknowledgments
The Publishers would like to thank the following for permission to reproduce photographs:
Ace Photo Agency: Geoff Smith p. 8; Aviemore Photographic: p. 27; Bubbles: Pauline Cutler p. 14; Collections: Gena Davies p. 6, Roger Scruton p. 12; Images Color Library: pp. 5, 7; J. Allan Cash: pp. 11, 15, 17, 19, 21, 22, 23, 24, 26, 29; Link: Orde Eliason p. 16, Sue Carpenter p. 25; Shakespeare's Globe: p. 28; The Anthony Blake Photo Library: Gerrit Buntrock p. 13; The Skyscan Photolibrary: p. 10; Tony Stone Images: Penny Tweedie p. 20; Trip: P. Rauter p. 9, C. Kapolka p. 18.

Cover photograph reproduced with permission of Tony Stone Images/Peter Cade.

Every effort has been made to contact copyright holders of any material reproduced in this book. Any omissions will be rectified in subsequent printings if notice is given to the Publisher.

Any words appearing in bold, **like this**, are explained in the Glossary.

Contents

The United Kingdom

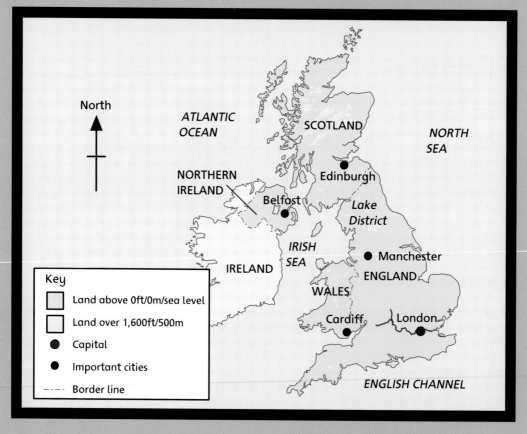

The United Kingdom is in Europe. It is made up of four parts. They are England, Northern Ireland, Scotland, and Wales.

Most people call the United Kingdom "the U.K.," for short. The people of the U.K. go to school, enjoy music, and live in homes like you. Life in the U.K. is **unique,** too.

Land

The north of the U.K. has mountains and deep valleys and lakes. In the south, there are gentle hills with wide rivers. It is easier to grow **crops** in the south.

There is lots of rain on the high land in the west of the U.K. Rain makes the grass and plants grow well.

Landmarks

The Giant's Causeway in Northern Ireland is an unusual **volcanic** rock on the coast. **Legend** says it was a giant's road built to cross over the sea into Scotland.

London is the **capital** of the U.K. It has
many famous buildings. The Tower of
London was once a prison castle. Today
many **tourists** visit the Tower of London to
see its **keepers** and the **crown jewels**.

Homes

Most people in the U.K. live in houses in towns or cities. Many of these houses were built more than 100 years ago.

Some people live in apartment buildings.
New apartments are being built, and some
empty, old buildings in the center of the
city are being made into apartments.

Food

There is a fish and chip shop in every town. Another name for chips is french fries. Because the U.K. is an island, there is fresh fish all year round.

Different parts of the U.K. have their own special dishes. Many families enjoy a **traditional** Sunday lunch. This meal is a big roast of meat with potatoes, vegetables, and **gravy**.

Clothes

Many famous **fashion designers** come
from the U.K. Young people enjoy wearing
clothes made by these top designers.
Sports clothes are also very popular.

One of the **traditional** clothes in the U.K. is the tartan kilt. This is a checked, wool skirt worn by Scottish men and women on special occasions.

Work

Seven out of ten people in the U.K. work in a service industry. They work in transportation, **education**, health, entertainment, or **finance**.

Most other people work in industry. They help to make or build things, such as cars. Very few people work in farming in the U.K.

Transportation

The London Underground is a subway
train system. It used **steam engines** 100
years ago. Now it runs by electricity.
Three million people travel on it every day.

Most people travel to work by car. Goods are hauled by truck. The roads and highways in the U.K. are very busy. This causes **pollution**.

Language

English is the most spoken language in the world. But in the U.K., English might sound different in each area because people speak with different **accents**.

In the U.K., about one million people speak Welsh, and some people speak **Gaelic**. Some people speak other languages because their parents or grandparents came from other countries.

School

Children go to school from the age of 5 until they are 16 years old. They study science, geography, history, English, music, math, art, and physical education.

Most children go to a local, free school.
Some families pay money for their
children to attend school. Some children
live at their school during the school year.

Free Time

Many sports began in the U.K., such as soccer, tennis, and a baseball-like game called cricket. Children play and watch these games in and out of school.

Many people enjoy being outdoors. Some go to the beach in summer. Others walk or ride a bicycle in the mountains.

Celebrations

The biggest celebration of the year is Christmas. The streets are bright with colorful lights. People buy presents for each other. They eat special Christmas food.

Another special celebration is Burn's Night
in Scotland. People wear tartan clothes and
eat a special food called haggis. They listen
to **bagpipe** music.

The Arts

The U.K. is famous for its theater. **William Shakespeare's** plays, written long ago, are known around the world. Also, there are many theaters and theater festivals.

The U.K. has many musicians and pop music groups. The Eisteddfod festival in Wales is a competition for singers, poets, and musicians.

Fact File

Name	The full name of the U.K. is the United Kingdom of Great Britain and Northern Ireland.
Capital	The **capital** city of the United Kingdom is London.
Language	Most people speak English, but some also speak Welsh or Gaelic.
Population	There are about 58 million people living in the United Kingdom.
Money	The English have the pound (£), which is divided into 100 pence. The Irish pound is called a punt. Scotland and Wales also have their own coins and bank notes.
Religion	There are many Christians in the United Kingdom, as well as Muslims, Sikhs, Hindus, Jews, and Buddhists.
Products	The United Kingdom produces oil and gas, wheat and other foods, chemicals, and cars and other transportation machinery.

Words You Can Learn

These words are Welsh.

diolch (DEE-olkh)	thank you
bore da (boh-re-DAR)	good morning
nos da (norse-dar)	good night
hwyl fawr (hooeel-vowr)	goodbye
ie (EE-eh)	yes
na (nar)	no

Glossary

accent	a way of saying words in an area of a country
bagpipes	a musical instrument that you blow. It has pipes and a bag to collect the air.
capital	the city where the government has its headquarters
crop	a plant that farmers grow and harvest (gather)
crown jewels	the crowns and special jewels worn by Kings and Queens of Great Britain
education	anything to do with teaching children or adults
fashion designer	a person who draws ideas for clothes
finance	business that has to do with money
Gaelic	the ancient language of the people who first lived in Ireland, Wales, and Breton in France
gravy	meat juices that are made into a sauce
keeper	person who wears special clothes and protects a building
legend	a well-known, old story which may or may not be true
pollution	dirt and smoke in the air, often made by car and truck engines
William Shakespeare	an English writer who lived more than 400 years ago. His plays and poems are still popular.
steam engine	a type of train engine that burned coal to make steam to make the train go
tourist	a person who is traveling for pleasure
traditional	the way things have been done or made for a long time
unique	different in a special way
volcanic	a type of melted rock that is pushed out from beneath the earth's surface

31

Index

More Books to Read

Arnold, Helen. *Great Britain*. Chatham, NJ: Raintree Steck-Vaughn Publishers. 1994.

Flint, David. *The United Kingdom*. Chatham, NJ: Raintree Steck-Vaughn Publishers. 1994. An older reader can help you with this book.

Parker, Lewis K. *England*. Vero Beach, FL: Rourke Book Company, Inc. 1994. An older reader can help you with this book.